The Little Book
of
Love

This is a Parragon book
This edition published in 2005

Parragon
Queen Street House
4 Queen Street
Bath BA1 1HE, UK

ISBN 1-40546-223-X

A copy of the British Library Cataloguing-in-Publication Data is
available from the British Library

Printed in China

The Little Book
of
Love

~ ❧ ~

p

Introduction

Romeo and Juliet are the world's most famous lovers. Although most of our love affairs aren't quite as dramatic in outcome as theirs, we can sympathize with the classic stages of their romance since, while we all feel our affairs are uniquely intense, we also sense the universality of our emotions. Many of us try to express that feeling with some touching lines of poetry. Most of us, though good on the unique, are less successful at capturing the universal. Here is a broad selection of some of the poets who were more successful.

Love is Like a Dizziness

O, Love, love, love!
Love is like a dizziness;
It winna let a poor body
Gang about his biziness!
James Hogg 1770 – 1835

A Red, Red Rose

O my Love's like a red, red rose,
That's newly sprung in June;
O my Love's like the melodie
That's sweetly play'd in tune –

As fair art thou, my bonnie lass,
So deep in love am I;
And I will love thee still, my Dear,
Till a' the seas gang dry –

Till a' the seas gang dry, my Dear,
And the rocks melt wi' the sun:
I will love thee still, my Dear,
While the sands o' life shall run –

And fare thee well, my only Love!
And fare thee well, a while!
And I will come again, my Love,
Tho' it were ten thousand mile!

Robert Burns   1759 – 96

First Love

I ne'er was struck before that hour
With love so sudden and so sweet
Her face it bloomed like a sweet flower
And stole my heart away complete
My face turned pale a deadly pale
My legs refused to walk away
And when she looked what could I ail
My life and all seemed turned to clay

And then my blood rushed to my face
And took my eyesight quite away
The trees and bushes round the place
Seemed midnight at noon day
I could not see a single thing
Words from my eyes did start
They spoke as chords do from the string
And blood burnt round my heart

Are flowers the winter's choice
Is love's bed always snow
She seemed to hear my silent voice
Not loves appeals to know

I never saw so sweet a face
As that I stood before
My heart has left its dwelling place
And can return no more –

John Clare 1793–1864

Sonnet *from the* Portuguese XIV

If thou must love me, let it be for nought
Except for love's sake only. Do not say
'I love her for her smile … her look … her way
Of speaking gently, – for a trick of thought
That falls in well with mine, and certes brought
A sense of pleasant ease on such a day' –
For these things in themselves, Beloved, may
be changed, or change for thee, – and love, so wrought
May be unwrought so. Neither love me for
Thine own dear pity's wiping my cheeks dry,
Since one might well forget to weep who bore
Thy comfort long, and lose thy love thereby.
But love me for love's sake, that evermore
Thou may'st love on through love's eternity.

Elizabeth Barrett Browning   1806 – 61

Song

Go, lovely rose –
Tell her that wastes her time and me,
That now she knows,
When I resemble her to thee
How sweet and fair she seems to be.

Tell her that's young,
And shuns to have her graces spied,
That hadst thou sprung
In deserts where no men abide,
Thou must have uncommended died.

Small is the worth
Of beauty from the light retired:
Bid her come forth,
Suffer herself to be desired,
And not blush so to be admired.

Then die! – that she
The common fate of all things rare
May read in thee;
How small a part of time they share
That are so wondrous sweet and fair!

Edmund Waller   1606 – 87

To My Heavenly Charmer

My poor expecting Heart beats for thy Breast,
In ev'ry pulse, and will not let me rest;
A thousand dear Desires are waking there,
Whose softness will not a Description bear,
Oh! let me pour them to thy lovely eyes,
And catch their tender meanings as they rise.
My ev'ry Feature with my Passion glows
In ev'ry thought and look it overflows.
Too noble and too strong for all Disguise,
It rushes from my love-discov'ring Eyes.
Nor Rules nor Reason can my Love restrain;
Its godlike Tide runs high in ev'ry Vein.
To the whole World my Tenderness be known,
What is the World to her, who lives for thee alone.

Martha Sansom 1690 – 1736

A Picture

It was in autumn that I met
Her whom I love; the sunflowers bold
Stood up like guards around her set,
And all the air with mignonette
Was warm within the garden old;
Beside her feet the marigold
Glowed star-like, and the sweet-pea sent
A sigh to follow as she went
Slowly adown the terrace; – there
I saw thee, oh my love! and thou wert fair.

She stood in the full noonday, unafraid,
As one beloved of sunlight, for awhile
She leant upon the timeworn balustrade;
The white clematis wooed her, and the clove
Hung all its burning heart upon her smile;
And on her cheek and in her eyes was love;
And on her lips that, like an opening rose,
Seemed parting some sweet secret to disclose,
The soul of all the summer lingered; – there
I saw thee, oh my love! and thou wert fair.

Dora Greenwell 1821 – 82

Oh Lift Me!

Oh lift me from the grass!
I die! I faint! I fail!
Let thy love and kisses rain
On my lips and eyelids pale.
My cheek is cold and white, alas!
My heart beats loud and fast: –
Oh! Press it to thine own again,
Where it will break at last.

Percy Bysshe Shelley 1792 – 1822

from Hero and Leander

It lies not in our power to love or hate
For will in us is over-ruled by fate.
When two are stripped, long ere the course begin,
We wish that one should lose, the other win;
And one especially do we affect
Of two gold ingots, like in each respect.
The reason no man knows; let it suffice,
What we behold is censured by our eyes.
Where both deliberate, the love is slight;
Who ever loved, that loved not at first sight?

Christopher Marlowe 1564 – 93

To Cupid

Child, with many a childish wile,
Timid look, and blushing smile,
Downy wings to steal thy way,
Gilded bow, and quiver gay,
Who in thy simple mien would trace
The tyrant of the human race?
Who is he whose flinty heart
Hath not felt the flying dart?
Who is he that from the wound
Hath not pain and pleasure found?
Who is he that hath not shed
Curse and blessing on thy head?

Joanna Baillie   1762 – 1851

Sonnet 113

Since I left you, mine eye is in my mind,
And that which governs me to go about
Doth part his function and is partly blind,
Seems seeing, but effectually is out;
For it no form delivers to the heart
Of bird, of flower, or shape, which it doth latch:
Of his quick objects hath the mind no part.
Nor his own vision holds what it doth catch;
For if it see the rudest or gentlest sight,
The most sweet favour or deformed'st creature,
The mountain or the sea, the day or night,
The crow or dove, it shapes them to your feature:
Incapable of more, replete with you,
My most true mind thus maketh mine untrue.

William Shakespeare 1564 – 1616

A Moment

The clouds had made a crimson crown
Above the mountains high.
The stormy sun was going down
In a stormy sky.

Why did you let your eyes so rest on me,
And hold your breath between?
In all the ages this can never be
As if it had not been.

Mary Elizabeth Coleridge 1861 – 1907

The Look

Strephon kissed me in the spring,
Robin in the fall,
But Colin only looked at me
And never kissed at all.

Strephon's kiss was lost in jest,
Robin's lost in play,
But the kiss in Colin's eyes
Haunts me night and day.

Sara Teasdale 1884 – 1933

Sonnet

I wish I could remember that first day,
First hour, first moment of your meeting me.
If bright or dim the season, it might be
Summer or Winter for aught that I can say:
So unrecorded did it slip away,
So blind was I to see and to foresee,
So dull to mark the budding of my tree
That would not blossom yet for many a May.
If only I could recollect it, such
A day of days! I let it come and go
As traceless as a thaw of bygone snow;
It seemed to mean so little, meant so much;
If only now I could recall that touch,
First touch of hand in hand. – Did one but know!

Christina Rossetti 1830 – 94

from Aire and Angels

Twice or thrice had I lov'd thee,
Before I knew thy face or name;
So in a voice, so in a shapelesse flame,
Angels affect us oft, and worship'd be;
Still when, to where thou wert, I came,
Some lovely glorious nothing I did see.
But since my soule, whose child love is,
Takes limmes of flesh, and else could nothing doe,
More subtile than the parent is,
Love must not be, but take a body too,
And therefore what thou wert, and who,
I bid Love aske, and now
That it assume thy body, I allow,
And fixe it selfe in thy lip, eye, and brow.

John Donne 1572 – 1631

Stanzas

~ ✦ ~

Oh, come to me in dreams, my love!
I will not ask a dearer bliss;
Come with the starry beams, my love,
And press mine eyelids with thy kiss.

'Twas thus, as ancient fables tell,
Love visited a Grecian maid,
Till she disturbed the sacred spell,
And woke to find her hopes betrayed.

But gentle sleep shall veil my sight,
And Psyche's lamp shall darkling be,
When, in the visions of the night,
Thou dost renew thy vows to me.

Then come to me in dreams, my love,
I will not ask a dearer bliss;
Come with the starry beams, my love,
And press mine eyelids with thy kiss.

Mary Wollstonecraft Shelley 1797 – 1851

And On My Eyes Dark Sleep By Night

Come, dark-eyed Sleep, thou child of Night,
Give me thy dreams, thy lies;
Lead through the horny portal white
The pleasure day denies.

O bring the kiss I could not take
From lips that would not give;
Bring me the heart I could not break,
The bliss for which I live.

I care not if I slumber blest
By fond delusion; nay,
Put me on Phaon's lips to rest,
And cheat the cruel day!

Michael Field   1846 – 1914

From the Telephone

Out of the dark cup
Your voice broke like a flower.
It trembled, swaying on its taut stem.
The caress in its touch
Made my eyes close.

Florence Ripley Mastin late 19th century

How Long Shall I Pine?

How long shall I pine for love?
How long shall I muse in vain?
How long like the turtle-dove
Shall I heavenly thus complain?
Shall the sails of my love stand still?
Shall the grists of my hopes be unground?
Oh fie, oh fie, oh fie,
Let the mill, let the mill go round.

John Fletcher 1579 – 1625

All Thoughts, All Passions

All thoughts, all passions, all delights,
Whatever stirs this mortal frame,
All are but ministers of Love,
And feed his sacred flame.

Samuel Taylor Coleridge 1772 – 1834

Youth and Beauty

Thou art so fair, and young withal,
Thou kindl'st young desires in me,
Restoring life to leaves that fall,
And sight to eyes that hardly see
Half those fresh beauties bloom in thee.

Those, under sev'ral herbs and flow'rs
Disguis'd, were all Medea gave,
When she recall'd time's flying hours,
And aged Aeson from his grave,
For beauty can both kill and save.

Youth it enflames, but age it cheers,
I would go back, but not return
To twenty but to twice those years;
Not blaze, but ever constant burn,
For fear my cradle prove my urn.

Aurelian Townshend 1583 – 1643

The Vain Advice

Ah, gaze not on those eyes! forbear
That soft enchanting voice to hear:
Not looks of basilisks give surer death,
Nor Syrens sing with more destructive breath.

Fly, if thy freedom thoud'st maintain,
Alas! I feel th'advice is vain!
A heart whose safety but in flight does lie,
Is too far lost to have the power to fly.

Catherine Cockburn 1679 – 1749

On His Mistress, the Queen of Bohemia

You meaner beauties of the night,
That poorly satisfy our eyes
More by your number than your light,
You common people of the skies;
What are you when the moon shall rise?

You curious chanters of the wood,
That warble forth Dame Nature's lays,
Thinking your passions understood
By your weak accents; what's your praise,
When Philomel her voice shall raise?

You violets that first appear,
By your pure purple mantles known
Like the proud virgins of the year,
As if the spring were all your own;
What are you when the rose is blown?

So, when my mistress shall be seen
In form and beauty of her mind,
By virtue first, then choice, a Queen,
Tell me if she were not designed
Th' eclipse and glory of her kind.

Sir Henry Wotton   1568 – 1639

29

At a Dinner Party

With fruit and flowers the board is decked,
The wine and laughter flow;
I'll not complain – could one expect
So dull a world to know?

You look across the fruit and flowers,
My glance your glances find. –
It is our secret, only ours,
Since all the world is blind.

Amy Levy   1861 – 89

To Celia

Drink to me, onely, with thine eyes,
And I will pledge with mine;
Or leave a kisse but in the cup,
And I'll not look for wine.
The thirst that from the soule doth rise,
Doth aske a drink divine:
But might I of Jove's Nectar sup,
I would not change for thine.
I sent thee, late, a rosie wreath,
Not so much honoring thee,
As giving it a hope, that there
It could not withered bee.
But thou thereon did'st onely breathe,
And sent'st it backe to me:
Since when it growes, and smells, I sweare,
Not of it self, but thee.

Ben Jonson 1572 – 1637

Live With Me

Live with me, and be my love,
And we will all the pleasure prove
That hills and valleys, dales and fields,
And all the craggy mountains yields.

There will we sit upon the rocks,
And see the shepherds feed their flocks
By shallow rivers, by whose falls
Melodious birds sing madrigals.

There will I make thee a bed of roses,
With a thousand fragrant posies,
A cap of flowers, and a kirtle
Embroider'd all with leaves of myrtle.

A belt of straw and ivy buds
With coral clasps and amber studs,
And if these pleasures may thee move,
Then live with me and be my love.

Anon   16th century

A Lover's Plea

Shall I come, sweet Love, to thee,
When the evening beams are set?
Shall I not excluded be?
Will you find no feigned let?
Let me not, for pity, more
Tell the long hours at your door.

Who can tell what thief or foe
In the covert of the night
For his prey will work my woe,
Or through wicked foul despite?
So may I die unredressed,
Ere my long love be possessed.

But to let such dangers pass,
Which a lover's thoughts disdain,
'Tis enough in such a place
To attend love's joys in vain.
Do not mock me in thy bed,
While these cold nights freeze me dead.

Thomas Campion   1567 – 1620

O Mistress Mine, *from* Twelfth Night

O mistress mine, where are you roaming?
O stay and hear, your true love's coming,
That can sing both high and low.
Trip no further, pretty sweeting.
Journeys end in lovers meeting,
Every wise man's son doth know.
What is love? 'tis not hereafter,
Present mirth, hath present laughter:
What's to come is still unsure.
In delay there lies no plenty,
Then come kiss me, sweet and twenty:
Youth's a stuff will not endure.

William Shakespeare 1564 – 1616

Once We Played

Once we played at love together –
Played it smartly, if you please;
Lightly, as a windblown feather,
Did we stake a heart apiece.

Oh, it was delicious fooling!
In the hottest of the game,
Without thought of future cooling,
All too quickly burned Life's flame.

In this give-and-take of glances,
Kisses sweet as honey dews,
When we played with equal chances,
Did you win, or did I lose?

Mathilde Blind   1841 – 96

Plain as the Glistering Planets Shine

Plain as the glistering planets shine
When winds have cleaned the skies,
Her love appeared, appealed for mine,
And wantoned in her eyes.

Clear as the shining tapers burned
On Cytherea's shrine,
Those brimming, lustrous beauties turned,
And called and conquered mine.

The beacon-lamp that Hero lit
No fairer shone on sea,
No plainlier summoned will and wit,
Than hers encouraged me.

I thrilled to feel her influence near,
I struck my flag at sight.
Her starry silence smote my ear
Like sudden drums at night.

I ran as, at the cannon's roar,
The troops the ramparts man –

As in the holy house of yore
The willing Eli ran.

Here, lady, lo! that servant stands
You picked from passing men,
And should you need not heart nor hands
He bows and goes again.

Robert Louis Stevenson   1850 – 94

To ...

One word is too often profaned
For me to profane it;
One feeling too falsely disdained
For thee to disdain it;
One hope is too like despair
For prudence to smother;
And pity from thee more dear
Than that from another.

I can give not what men call love:
But wilt thou accept not
The worship the heart lifts above
And the heavens reject not,
The desire of the moth for the star,
Of the night for the morrow,
The devotion to something afar
From the sphere of our sorrow?

Percy Bysshe Shelley 1792 – 1822

Love Me at Last

Love me at last, or if you will not,
Leave me;
Hard words could never, as these half-words,
Grieve me:
Love me at last – or leave me.

Love me at last, or let the last word uttered
Be but your own;
Love me, or leave me – as a cloud, a vapor,
Or a bird flown.
Love me at last – I am but sliding water
Over a stone.

Alice Corbin late 19th century

from A Fragment

For when in floods of Love we're drench'd,
The flames are by enjoyment quench'd:
But thus, let's thus together lie,
And kiss out long Eternity:
Here we dread no conscious spies,
No blushes stain our guiltless Joys:
Here no Faintness dulls Desires,
And Pleasure never flags, nor tires:
This has pleas'd, and pleases now,
And for Ages will do so:
Enjoyment here is never down,
But fresh, and always but begun.

Petronius   1st century AD

from Twelfth Night *Act I Scene v*

Make me a willow cabin at your gate,
And call upon my soul within the house;
Write loyal cantons of contemned love,
And sing them loud even in the dead of night;
Holla your name to the reverberate hills,
And make the babbling gossip of the air
Cry out 'Olivia!' O! you should not rest
Between the elements of air and earth,
But you should pity me!

William Shakespeare 1564–1616

I'll Never Love Thee More

My dear and only love, I pray
That little world of thee
Be governed by no other sway
Than purest monarchy;
For if confusion have a part
(Which virtuous should abhor),
And hold a synod in thine heart,
I'll never love thee more.

Like Alexander I will reign,
And I will reign alone;
My thoughts did evermore disdain
A rival on my throne.
He either fears his fate too much,
Or his deserts are small,
That dares not put it to the touch,
To gain or lose it all.

And in the empire of thine heart,
Where I should solely be,
If others do pretend a part
Or dare to vie with me,

Or if Committees thou erect,
And go on such a score,
I'll laugh and sing at thy neglect,
And never love thee more.

But if thou wilt prove faithful then,
And constant of thy word,
I'll make thee glorious by my pen
And famous by my sword;
I'll serve thee in such noble ways
Was never heard before;
I'll crown and deck thee all with bays,
And love thee more and more.

James Graham, Marquis of Montrose 1612 – 56

Beauty

Let us use it while we may;
Snatch those joys that haste away.
Earth her winter-coat may cast,
And renew her beauty past;
But, our winter come, in vain
We solicit spring again:
And when our furrows snow shall cover,
Love may return, but never lover.

Sir Richard Fanshawe 1608 – 66
(from the Italian of Giovanni Battista Guarini)

To Minnie

A picture-frame for you to fill,
A paltry setting for your face,
A thing that has no worth until
You lend it something of your grace,

I send (unhappy I that sing
Laid by awhile upon the shelf)
Because I would not send a thing
Less charming than you are yourself.

And happier than I, alas!
(Dumb thing, I envy its delight)
'Twill wish you well, the looking-glass,
And look you in the face to-night.

Robert Louis Stevenson   1850 – 94

To his Coy Mistress

Had we but world enough, and time,
This coyness, Lady, were no crime.
We would sit down and think which way
To walk and pass our long love's day.
Thou by the Indian Ganges' side
Should'st rubies find: I by the tide
Of Humber would complain. I would
Love you ten years before the flood,
And you should, if you please, refuse
Till the conversion of the Jews.
My vegetable love should grow
Vaster than empires, and more slow.
An hundred years should go to praise
Thine eyes and on thy forehead gaze;
Two hundred to adore each breast,
But thirty thousand to the rest.
An age at least to every part,
And the last age should show your heart.
For, Lady, you deserve this state,
Nor would I love at lower rate.
But at my back I always hear
Time's winged chariot hurrying near;

And yonder all before us lie
Deserts of vast eternity.
Thy beauty shall no more be found,
Nor, in my marble vault, shall sound
My echoing song: then worms shall try
That long preserved virginity,
And your quaint honour turn to dust,
And into ashes all my lust.
The grave's a fine and private place
But none, I think, do there embrace.
Now therefore, while the youthful hue
Sits on thy skin like morning dew,
And while thy willing soul transpires
At every pore with instant fires,
Now let us sport us while we may,
And now, like amorous birds of prey,
Rather at once our time devour
Than languish in his slow-chapt power.
Let us roll all our strength and all
Our sweetness up into one ball,
And tear our pleasures with rough strife
Through the iron gates of life:
Thus, though we cannot make our sun
Stand still, yet we will make him run.

Andrew Marvell 1621 – 78

47

Love's Philosophy

The fountains mingle with the river
And the rivers with the ocean,
The winds of heaven mix for ever
With a sweet emotion;
Nothing in the world is single,
All things by a law divine
In one another's being mingle –
Why not I with thine?

See the mountains kiss high heaven
And the waves clasp one another;
No sister-flower would be forgiven
If it disdain'd its brother:

And the sunlight clasps the earth,
And the moonbeams kiss the sea –
What are all these kissings worth,
If thou kiss not me?

Percy Bysshe Shelley   1792 – 1822

One Day I Wrote Her Name

One day I wrote her name upon the strand,
But came the waves and washed it away:
Again I wrote it with a second hand,
But came the tide, and made my pains his prey.
Vain man, said she, that dost in vain assay
A mortal thing so to immortalize,
For I myself shall like to this decay,
And eke my name be wiped out likewise.
Not so, (quod I) let baser things devise
To die in dust, but you shall live by fame:
My verse your virtues rare shall eternize,
And in the heavens write your glorious name:
Where, whenas Death shall all the world subdue,
Our love shall live, and later life renew.

Edmund Spenser 1552 – 99

Sonnet 18

Shall I compare thee to a summer's day?
Thou art more lovely and more temperate:
Rough winds do shake the darling buds of May,
And summer's lease hath all too short a date:
Sometime too hot the eye of heaven shines,
And often is his gold complexion dimm'd,
And every fair from fair sometime declines,
By chance, or nature's changing course untrimm'd:
But thy eternal summer shall not fade,
Nor lose possession of that fair thou owest,
Nor shall death brag thou wandrest in his shade,
When in eternal lines to time thou growest,
So long as men can breathe, or eyes can see
So long lives this, and this gives life to thee.

William Shakespeare 1564 – 1616

To My Dear and Loving Husband

If ever two were one, then surely we.
If ever man were lov'd by wife, then three.
If ever wife was happy in a man,
Compare with me, ye woman, if you can.
I prize thy love more than whole mines of gold,
Or all the riches that the east doth hold.
My love is such that rivers cannot quench,
Nor ought but love from thee give recompence.
Thy love is such I can no way repay;
The heavens reward thee manifold I pray.
Then while we live, in love let's so persevere,
That when we love no more, we may live ever.

Anne Bradstreet 1612 – 72

Song

Nay but you, who do not love her,
Is she not pure gold, my mistress?
Holds earth aught – speak truth – above her?
Aught like this tress, see, and this tress,
And this last fairest tress of all,
So fair, see, ere I let it fall?

Because, you spend your lives in praising;
To praise, you search the wide world over:
So, why not witness, calmly gazing,
If earth holds aught – speak truth – above her?
Above this tress, and this I touch
But cannot praise, I love so much!

Robert Browning 1812 – 89

Happy Marriage

Thou genius of connubial love, attend!
Let silent wonder all thy powers suspend,
Whilst to thy glory I devote my lays,
And pour forth all my grateful heart in praise.
In lifeless strains let vulgar satire tell
That marriage oft is mixed with heaven and hell,
That conjugal delight is soured with spleen,
And peace and war compose the varied scene.
My muse a truth sublimer can assert,
And sing the triumphs of a mutual heart.

Thrice happy they who through life's varied tide
With equal pace and gentle motion glide,
Whom, though the wave of fortune sinks or swells,
One reason governs and one wish impels,
Whose emulation is to love the best,
Who feels no bliss but in each other blest,
Who knows no pleasure but the joys they give,
Nor cease to love but when they cease to live.
If fate these blessings in one lot combine,
Then let th'eternal page record them mine.

Thomas Blacklock 1721 – 91

Sonnet 29

When in disgrace with fortune and men's eyes,
I all alone beweep my out-cast state,
And trouble deaf heaven with my bootless cries,
And look upon myself, and curse my fate,
Wishing me like to one more rich in hope,
Featur'd like him, like him with friends possess'd,
Desiring this man's art, and that man's scope,
With what I most enjoy contented least,
Yet in these thoughts myself almost despising,
Haply I think on thee, – and then my state,
Like to the lark at break of day arising
From sullen earth, sings hymns at heaven's gate;
For thy sweet love rememb'red such wealth brings
That then I scorn to change my state with kings.

William Shakespeare   1564 – 1616

No Other Choice

Fain would I change that note
To which fond Love hath charmed me
Long, long to sing by rote,
Fancying that that harmed me:
Yet when this thought doth come,
'Love is the perfect sum
Of all delight,'
I have no other choice
Either for pen or voice
To sing or write.

O Love! they wrong thee much
That say thy sweet is bitter,
When thy rich fruit is such
As nothing can be sweeter.
Fair house of joy and bliss,
Where truest pleasure is,
I do adore thee:
I know thee what thou art,
I serve thee with my heart,
And fall before thee.

Anon late 16th century

The Bargain

My true love hath my heart, and I have his,
By just exchange, one for the other given
I hold his dear, and mine he cannot miss,
There never was a better bargain driven.
His heart in me keeps me and him in one,
My heart in him his thoughts and senses guides;
He loves my heart, for once it was his own,
I cherish his, because in me it bides.
His heart his wound received from my sight,
My heart was wounded with his wounded heart;
For as from me on him his hurt did light,
So still methought in me his hurt did smart.
Both equal hurt, in this change sought our bliss:
My true love hath my heart and I have his.

Sir Philip Sidney   1554 – 86

The Summer

The Summer hath his joys,
And Winter his delights.
Though Love and all his pleasures are but toys,
They shorten tedious nights.

Thomas Campion 1567–1620

from My Beloved Is Mine and I Am His

Nor Time, nor Place, nor Chance, nor Death can bow
My least desires unto the least remove;
He's firmly mine by Oath; I, His, by Vow;
He's mine by Faith, and I am His by Love;
He's mine by Water; I am His by Wine;
Thus I my Best-Beloved's am; thus He is mine.

He is my Altar; I, his Holy Place;
I am his Guest; and he, my living Food;
I'm his, by Penitence; He, mine by Grace;
I'm his, by Purchase; He is mine, by Blood;
He's my supporting Elm, and I, his Vine:
Thus I my Best-Beloved's am; thus He is mine.

He gives me wealth, I give him all my Vowes:
I give him songs; He gives me length of dayes:
With wreathes of Grace he crownes my conqu'ring brow
And I his Temples, with a Crowne of Praise,
Which he accepts as an ev'rlasting signe,
That I my Best-Beloved's am; that He is mine.

Francis Quarles 1592–1644

A Birthday

My heart is like a singing bird
Whose nest is in a watered shoot;
My heart is like a rainbow shell
That paddles in a halcyon sea;
My heart is gladder than all these
Because my love is come to me.

Raise me a dais of silk and down;
Hang it with vair and purple dyes;
Carve it in doves and pomegranates
And peacocks with a hundred eyes;
Work it in gold and silver grapes,
In leaves and silver fleurs-de-lys;
Because the birthday of my life
Is come, my love is come to me.

Christina Rossetti 1830 – 94

Those Who Love

Those who love the most,
Do not talk of their love,
Francesca, Guinevere,
Deirdre, Iseult, Heloise,
In the fragrant gardens of heaven
Are silent, or speak if at all
Of fragile inconsequent things.

And a woman used to know
Who loved one man from her youth,
Against the strength of the fates
Fighting in somber pride
Never spoke of this thing,
But hearing his name by chance,
A light would pass over her face.

Sara Teasdale 1884 – 1933

Lovesight

When do I see the most, beloved one?
When in the light the spirits of mine eyes
Before thy face, their altar, solemnize
The worship of that Love through thee made known?
Or when in the dusk hours, (we two alone,)
Close-kissed and eloquent of still replies
Thy twilight-hidden glimmering visage lies,
And my soul only sees thy soul its own?

O love, my love! if I no more should see
Thyself, nor on the earth the shadow of thee,
Nor image of thine eyes in any spring, –
How then should sound upon Life's darkening slope
The ground-whirl of the perished leaves of Hope,
The wind of Death's imperishable wing?

Dante Gabriel Rossetti 1828 – 82

Second Thoughts

I thought of leaving her for a day
In town, it was such iron winter
At Durdans, the garden frosty clay,
The woods as dry as any splinter,
The sky congested. I would break
From the deep, lethargic country air
To the shining lamps, to the clash of the play,
And to-morrow, wake
Beside her, a thousand things to say.
I planned – O more – I had almost started; –
I lifted her face in my hands to kiss, –
A face in a border of fox's fur,
For the bitter black wind had stricken her,
And she wore it – her soft hair straying out
Where it buttoned against the gray, leather snout;
In an instant we should have parted;
But at sight of the delicate world within
That fox-fur collar, from brow to chin,
At sight of those wonderful eyes from the mine,
Coal pupils, an iris of glittering spa,
And the wild, ironic, defiant shine
As of a creature behind a bar

One has captured, and, when three lives are past,
May hope to reach the heart of at last,
All that, and the love at her lips, combined
To shew me what folly it were to miss
A face with such thousand things to say,
And beside these, such thousand more to spare,
For the shining lamps, for the clash of the play –
O madness; not for a single day
Could I leave her! I stayed behind.

Michael Field   1846 – 1914

To Celia

Not, Celia, that I juster am
Or better than the rest!
For I would change each hour, like them,
Were not my heart at rest.

But I am tied to very thee
By every thought I have;
Thy face I only care to see,
Thy heart I only crave.

All that in woman is adored
In thy dear self I find –
For the whole sex can but afford
The handsome and the kind.

Why then should I seek further store,
And still make love anew?
When change itself can give no more,
'Tis easy to be true!

Sir Charles Sedley 1639 –1701

from O Lay Thy Hand in Mine

O lay thy hand in mine, dear!
We're growing old, we're growing old;
But Time hath brought no sign, dear,
That hearts grow cold, that hearts grow cold.
'Tis long, long since our new love
Made life divine, made life divine;
But age enricheth true love,
Like noble wine, like noble wine.

Gerald Massey 1828 – 1907

A Song

Love, thou art best of Human Joys,
Our chiefest Happiness below;
All other Pleasures are but Toys,
Music without Thee is but Noise,
And beauty but an empty show.

Heav'n, who knew best what Man wou'd move,
And raise his Thoughts above the Brute;
Said, Let him Be, and Let him Love;
That must alone his Soul improve,
Howe'er Philosophers dispute.

Ann Finch   1661 – 1720

Sonnet 116

Let me not to the marriage of true minds
Admit impediments. Love is not love
Which alters when it alteration finds,
Or bends with the remover to remove:
O, no, it is an ever-fixed mark,
That looks on tempests and is never shaken;
It is the star to every wandering bark,
Whose worth's unknown, although his height be taken.
Love's not Time's fool, though rosy lips and cheeks
Within his bending sickle's compass come;
Love alters not with his brief hours and weeks,
But bears it out even to the edge of doom.
If this be error and upon me proved,
I never writ, nor no man ever loved.

William Shakespeare 1564 – 1616

True Love

True Love is but a humble,
low-born thing,
And hath its food served up in
earthen ware:

It is a thing to walk with,
hand in hand,
Through the everydayness of
this workday world.

J. R. Lowell 1819 – 91

from Enough

Yet now, O Love, that you
Have kissed my forehead, I
Have sung indeed, can die,
And be forgotten too.

Digby Mackworth Dolben 1848 – 67

Last Sonnet

Bright Star! would I were steadfast as thou art –
Not in lone splendour hung aloft the night,
And watching, with eternal lids apart,
Like Nature's patient sleepless Eremite,
The moving waters at their priestlike task
Of pure ablution round earth's human shores,
Or gazing on the new soft-fallen mask
Of snow upon the mountains and the moors –
No – yet still steadfast, still unchangeable,
Pillow'd upon my fair love's ripening breast
To feel for ever its soft fall and swell,
Awake for ever in a sweet unrest;
Still, still to hear her tender-taken breath,
And so live ever – or else swoon to death.

John Keats 1795 –1821

The Constant Lover

Out upon it, I have loved
Three whole days together!
And am like to love three more,
If it hold fair weather.

Time shall moult away his wings
Ere he shall discover
In the whole wide world again
Such a constant lover.

But a pox upon't, no praise
There is due at all to me:
Love with me had made no stay,
Had it been any but she.

Had it any been but she,
And that very very face;
There had been at least ere this
A dozen dozen in her place.

Sir John Suckling   1609 – 41

Sonnet *from the* Portuguese XLIII

How do I love thee? Let me count the ways.
I love thee to the depth and breadth and height
My soul can reach, when feeling out of sight
For the ends of Being and ideal Grace.
I love thee to the level of everyday's
Most quiet need, by sun and candlelight.
I love thee freely, as men strive for Right;
I love thee purely, as they turn from Praise.
I love thee with the passion put to use
In my old griefs, and with my childhood's faith.
I love thee with a love I seemed to lose
With my lost saints, – I love thee with the breath,
Smiles, tears, of all my life! – and, if God choose,
I shall but love thee better after death.

Elizabeth Barrett Browning 1806 – 61

from By the Fireside

My perfect wife, my Leonor,
Oh, heart my own, oh eyes, mine too,
Whom else could I dare look backward for,
With whom beside should I dare pursue
The path grey heads abhor?

Robert Browning 1812 – 89

Loving in Truth

Loving in truth, and fain in verse my love to show,
That she, dear she, might take some pleasure of my pain:
Pleasure might cause her read, reading might make her know,
Knowledge might pity win, and pity grace obtain,
I sought fit words to paint the blackest face of woe,
Studying inventions fine, her wits to entertain:
Oft turning others' leaves to see if thence would flow
Some fresh and fruitful showers upon my sun-burn'd brain.
But words came halting forth, wanting Invention's stay,
Invention, Nature's child, fled step-dame Study's blows,
And others' feet still seem'd but strangers in my way.
Thus great with child to speak, and helpless in my throes,
Biting my trewand pen, beating myself for spite,
Fool, said my Muse to me, look in thy heart and write.

Sir Philip Sidney   1554 – 86

You Smiled, You Spoke

You smiled, you spoke, and I believed,
By every word and smile deceived.
Another man would hope no more;
Nor hope what I hoped before:
But let not this last wish be vain;
Deceive, deceive me once again!

Walter Savage Landor 1775–1864

The Slight

I did but crave that I might kiss
If not her lip, at least her hand,
The coolest Lover's frequent bliss,
And rude is she that will withstand
That inoffensive libertie;
She (would you think it?) in a fume
Turn'd her about and left the room,
Not she, she vow'd, not she.

Well Chariessa then said I,
If it must thus for ever be,
I can renounce my slavery,
And since you will not, can be free:
Many a time she made me dye,
Yet (would you think't?) I lov'd the more,
But I'le not tak't as heretofore,
Not I, I'le vow, not I.

Thomas Flatman   1635 – 88

Song

Why so pale and wan fond Lover?
Prithee why so pale?
Will, when looking well can't move her,
Looking ill prevaile?
Prithee why so pale?

Why so dull and mute young Sinner?
Prithee why so mute?
Will, when speaking well can't win her,
Saying nothing doo't?
Prithee why so mute?

Quit, quit, for shame, this will not move,
This will not take her;
If of her self she will not Love,
Nothing can make her:
The Devil take her.

Sir John Suckling 1609 – 41

R. Alcona to J. Brenzaida

Cold in the earth, and the deep snow piled above thee!
Far, far removed, cold in the dreary grave!
Have I forgot, my Only Love, to love thee,
Severed at last by Time's all-wearing wave?

Now, when alone, do my thoughts no longer hover
Over the mountains on Angora's shore;
Resting their wings where heath and fern-leaves cover
That noble heart for ever, ever more?

Cold in the earth, and fifteen wild Decembers
From those brown hills have melted into spring –
Faithful indeed is the spirit that remembers
After such years of change and suffering!

Sweet Love of youth, forgive if I forget thee
While the World's tide is bearing me along:
Sterner desires and darker hopes beset me,
Hopes which obscure but cannot do thee wrong.

No other sun has lightened up my heaven;
No other Star has ever shone for me:
All my life's bliss from thy dear life was given –
All my life's bliss is in the grave with thee.

But when the days of golden dreams had perished
And even Despair was powerless to destroy,
Then did I learn how existence could be cherished,
Strengthened and fed without the aid of joy;

Then did I check the tears of useless passion,
Weaned my young soul from yearning after thine;
Sternly denied its burning wish to hasten
Down to that tomb already more than mine!

And even yet, I dare not let it languish,
Dare not indulge in Memory's rapturous pain;
Once drinking deep of that divinest anguish,
How could I seek the empty world again?

Emily Bronte 1818 – 48

The Lost Love

She dwelt among the untrodden ways
Beside the springs of Dove;
A maid whom there were none to praise
And very few to love:

A violet by a mossy stone
Half-hidden from the eye!
– Fair as a star, when only one
Is shining in the sky.

She lived unknown, and few could know
When Lucy ceased to be;
But she is in her grave, and, oh,
The difference to me!

William Wordsworth 1770–1850

How Happy a Thing

How happy a thing were a wedding
And a bedding
If a man might purchase a wife
For a twelve month and a day;
But to live with her all a man's life,
For ever and for ay,
'Till she grow as grey as a cat,
Good faith, Mr Parson, I thank you for that.

Thomas Flatman 1635 – 88

So, We'll Go No More A-Roving

So, we'll go no more a-roving
So late into the night,
Though the heart be still as loving,
And the moon be still as bright.

For the sword outwears its sheath,
And the soul wears out the breast,
And the heart must pause to breathe,
And love itself have rest.

Though the night was made for loving,
And the day returns too soon,
Yet we'll go no more a-roving
By the light of the moon.

George Gordon, Lord Byron 1788–1824

Never Seek to Tell Thy Love

Never seek to tell thy love,
Love that never told can be;
For the gentle wind does move
Silently, invisibly.

I told my love, I told my love.
I told her all my heart,
Trembling, cold, in ghastly fears –
Ah, she doth depart.

Soon as she was gone from me
A traveller came by
Silently, invisibly –
He took her with a sigh. O, was no deny.

William Blake   1757 – 1827

The Secret

I loved thee, though I told thee not,
Right earlily and long,
Thou wert my joy in every spot,
My theme in every song.

And when I saw a stranger face
Where beauty held the claim,
I gave it like a secret grace
The being of thy name.

And all the charms of face or voice
Which I in others see
Are but the recollected choice
Of what I felt for thee.

John Clare 1793–1864

First Farewell to J.G.

Farewell my dearer half, joy of my heart,
Heaven only knows how loth I am to part:
Whole Months but hours seem, when you are here,
When absent, every Minute is a Year:
Might I but always see thy charming Face,
I'd live on Racks and wish no easier place.
But we must part, your Interest says we must;
Fate, me no longer with such Treasure trust.
I would not tax you with Inconstancy.
Yet Strephon, you are not so kind as I:
No interest, no nor Fate it self has pow'r
To tempt me from the Idol I adore:
But since you needs will go, may Africk be
Kinder to you, that Europe is to me:
May all you meet and every thing you view
Give out such Transport as I met in you.
May no sad thoughts disturb your quiet mind.
Except you'll think of her you left behind.

Ephelia 1678 – 82

Like the Touch of Rain

Like the touch of rain she was
On a man's flesh and hair and eyes
When the joy of walking thus
Has taken him by surprise:

With the love of the storm he burns,
He sings, he laughs, well I know how,
But forgets when he returns
As I shall not forget her 'Go now'.

Those two words shut a door
Between me and the blessed rain
That was never shut before
And will not open again.

Edward Thomas 1878–1917

Marriage

No more alone sleeping, no more alone waking
Thy dreams divided, thy prayers in twain;
Thy merry sisters tonight forsaking,
Never shall we see, maiden, again.

Never shall we see, thine eyes glancing,
Flashing with laughter and wild in glee
Under the mistletoe kissing and dancing,
Wantonly free.

There shall come a matron walking sedately,
Low-voiced, gentle, wise in reply.
Tell me, O tell me, can I love her greatly?
All for her sake must the maiden die!

Mary Coleridge 1861 – 1907

To J.G. on News of His Marriage

My Love? alas! I must not call you Mine,
But to your envy'd Bride that Name resign:
I must forget your lovely melting Charms,
And be forever Banisht from your Arms:
For ever? oh! the Horror of that Sound!
It gives my bleeding Heart a deadly wound:
While I might hope, although my Hope was vain,
It gave some Ease to my unpitty'd Pain,
But now your Hymen doth all Hope exclude,
And but to think is Sin, yet you intrude
On every thought; if I but close my Eyes,
Methinks your pleasing Form besides me lies;
With every Sigh I gently breathe your name,
Yet no ill thoughts pollute my hallow'd flame;
'Tis pure and harmless, as a Lambent Fire,
And never mingled with a warm Desire:
All I have now to ask of Bounteous Heaven,
Is, that your perjuries may be forgiven:
That she who you have with your Nuptials Blest,
As She's the Happiest Wife, may prove the best:
That all our Joys may light on you alone.

Then I can be contented to have none:
And never wish that you shoul'd kinder be,
Than now and then, to cast a Thought on Me:
And, Madam, though the Conquest you have won,
Over my Strephon, has my hopes undone:
I'le daily beg of Heaven, he may be
Kinder to You, than he has been to Me.

Ephelia 1678 – 82

Once Fondly Lov'd

Once fondly lov'd, and still remember'd dear,
Sweet early object of my youthful vows,
Accept this mark of friendship, warm, sincere –
Friendship! 'tis all cold duty now allows: –

And when you read the simple, artless rhymes,
One friendly sigh for him – he asks no more –
Who distant burns in flaming torrid climes,
Or haply lies beneath th' Atlantic roar.

Robert Burns   1759 – 96

Love and Friendship

Love is like the wild rose-briar,
Friendship like the holly tree –
The holly is dark when the rose-briar blooms
But which will bloom most constantly?

The wild rose-briar is sweet in spring,
Its summer blossoms scent the air;
Yet wait till winter comes again
And who will call the wild-briar fair?

Then scorn the silly rose-wreath now
And deck thee with the holly's sheen,
That when December blights thy brow
He still may leave thy garland green.

Emily Bronte   1818 – 48

Friendship After Love

After the fierce midsummer all ablaze
Has burned itself to ashes, and expires
In the intensity of its own fires,
There come the mellow, mild, St Martin days
Crowned with the calm of peace, but sad with haze.
So after Love has led us, till he tires
Of his own throes, and torments, and desires,
Comes large-eyed friendship: with a restful gaze,
He beckons us to follow, and across
Cool verdant vales we wander free from care.
Is it a touch of frost lies in the air?
Why are we haunted with a sense of loss?
We do not wish the pain back, or the heat;
And yet, and yet, these days are incomplete.

Ella Wheeler Wilcox 1850 – 1919

Sonnet

Tell me no more how fair she is,
I have no minde to hear
The story of that distant bliss
I never shall come near:
By sad experience I have found
That her perfection is my wound.

And tell me not how fond I am
To tempt a daring Fate,
From whence no triumph ever came,
But to repent too late:
There is some hope ere long I may
In silence dote my self away.

I ask no pity (Love) from thee,
Nor will thy justice blame,
So that thou wilt not envy mee
The glory of my flame:
Which crowns my heart when ere it dyes,
In that it falls her sacrifice.

Henry King   1592 – 1669

The Gift

What can I give you, my lord, my lover,
You who have given the world to me,
Showed me the light and the joy that cover
The wild sweet earth and the restless sea?

All that I have are gifts of your giving –
If I gave them again, you would find them old,
And your soul would weary of always living
Before the mirror my life would hold.

What shall I give you, my lord, my lover?
The gift that breaks the heart in me:
I bid you awake at dawn and discover
I have gone my way and left you free.

Sara Teasdale 1884–1933

Remember

Remember me when I am gone away,
Gone far away into the silent land;
When you can no more hold me by the hand,
Nor I half turn to go yet turning stay.
Remember me when no more day by day
You tell me of our future that you planned:
Only remember me; you understand
It will be late to counsel then or pray.
Yet if you should forget me for a while
And afterwards remember, do not grieve:
For if the darkness and corruption leave
A vestige of the thoughts that once I had,
Better by far you should forget and smile
Than that you should remember and be sad.

Christina Rossetti   1830 – 94

I Hold It True *from* In Memoriam

I hold it true, whate'er befall;
I feel it, when I sorrow most;
'Tis better to have loved and lost
Than never to have loved at all.

Alfred, Lord Tennyson 1809 – 92